Stories Told
in a Forgotten Tongue

poems by

Elaine Harootunian Reardon

Finishing Line Press
Georgetown, Kentucky

Stories Told
in a Forgotten Tongue

Copyright © 2024 by Elaine Harootunian Reardon
ISBN 979-8-88838-734-4 First Edition
All rights reserved under International and Pan-American Copyright Conventions. No part of this book may be reproduced in any manner whatsoever without written permission from the publisher, except in the case of brief quotations embodied in critical articles and reviews.

ACKNOWLEDGMENTS

The author wishes to acknowledge the following publications:

The Heart Is a Nursery for Hope: Canning Jars
Behind You: Assimilation, Refugee from Endearments, Quince Preserves.
North Dakota Quarterly: Copper Jazva.
Naugatuck River Review: Hye Holiday Gathering.
www.elainereardon.wordpress.com: Nesselrode Pudding.
Culinary Origami: What She Saved.
The Common: Morning Stories, Traveling to Marseille 1915.

Appreciation to grandmother Mariam for bringing her childhood alive through her morning stories and to others, like my cousin Vickie, who waited for drops of honey and cinnamon at the kitchen table. Also, appreciation to my long-time writing groups, The Kevin Higgins Faction, Galway, and The Ink Slingers, Dublin. I hope my grandchildren, Lina and Nico Martinez-Nocito, find something of themselves here.

Publisher: Leah Huete de Maines
Editor: Christen Kincaid
Cover Art: Watercolor *Venice Reflections* by Elaine Reardon from
       a Cindy Briggs Painting Workshop
Author Photo: James Toth
Cover Design: Elizabeth Maines McCleavy

Order online: www.finishinglinepress.com
       also available on amazon.com

Author inquiries and mail orders:
Finishing Line Press
PO Box 1626
Georgetown, Kentucky 40324
USA

Contents

Morning Stories 1

Copper Jazva 2

May 3

Assimilation 4

Kitchen 5

Canning Jars 6

Hye Holiday Gathering 7

Nesselrode Pudding 8

June Morning 9

Refugees from Endearments 10

October 12

What She Saved 13

An Early Snow 14

Traveling Through Marseille 15

Thanksgiving Choreg 16

Midnight Hunger 17

Quince Preserves 18

Late August 19

Keep In Mind 20

Morning Stories

When I woke in the morning
and begged for stories, Gram said
*don't talk, flies will get into your mouth.
After our work I'll tell you a story.*

She tied an apron around me,
pulled the stool to the table,
gave me parsley, cracked wheat,
ground lamb, a basin
of water to wet my hands.

She said *knead so it's
as soft as a baby's bottom.
Shape round smooth balls.*
We poked our thumbs in
to open them and spooned
in stuffing. I still wanted a story.

Gram said *my grandmother made kufta
with me, and I carried lunch to my grandpa
when he worked in the fields.* Sometimes
she rode the donkey, other times a horse.
Gram said *never ride a horse or a camel!*
And we never did, in our Boston neighborhood.

I watched her story unfold in my mind. On her
final day home she and her sisters returned home
from school and found the family murdered, the locked
church filled with men set on fire. A silent village now,
except for soldiers that gathered survivors.

They walked from their mountain village,
part of the desert death marches,
thirsty, eating grasses and weeds,
anything they found.
Two sisters fell in the desert,
three trudged on to Aleppo
and onward from there, survivors.

Copper Jazva

Gram read our coffee grounds only once
when my cousin and I were fifteen, ready to date.

She pulled out the jazva, brought the Turkish
coffee grounds to a foaming boil three times,

poured our cups full. She had never been
willing to tell fortunes before. We added

sugar and drank at the kitchen table in silence,
then turned our cups over to rest on saucers.

Coffee grounds dripped their fortune-telling
patterns down the china cups and Gram began.

She turned my cup over and paused. Surprised,
she said *mountains*, then she saw a *no good boy*,

someone new in my life. *Not worth anything.*
I was sure she was in cahoots with my dad

to keep me from dating. Gerry had begun walking
me home from school, and we had our first date.

A week later I found she was right about Gerry.
And now I live halfway up the mountain.

May

She plants skullcap, St John's wort,
and raspberry in the new garden.

She transplants bee balm behind
peonies, sets in thyme and chives.

She marks out rows of calendula,
lays in asparagus, and tends currants.

She welcomes bleeding hearts, wild daisies,
and yarrow that emerge without a care.

She's covered in mud, joyful
even as she swats mosquitos away.

Her daughter has long left home.
Even the cats have moved on now.

But each May wild strawberries and violets
return, rampaging through the lawn.

She sits on the screened porch
when it rains, listens to a thrush's song.

Assimilation

Immigration, assimilation,
sometimes it's how the tongue
and heart work in concert

to shape a new language, search
for work, green cards, or clothing.
My teachers were often confused

by the unusual Armenian-Irish
accent I brought from home. Friends
were baffled by foods in my lunch box.

We balance promises of America
on a seesaw. We can't recapture our
parents' past, we can only put one foot

in front of the other, walk into our own
present day, step by step. I wasn't a child
with pure blood. I had two races, three

languages, and lingering anguish from a forced
march from the mountain village through the desert
to Aleppo, and memories of a village I'll never see.

Kitchen

The old-fashioned once a week
down-on-your-knees, getting
into the lowest chair rungs
with a dust rag, followed
by furniture polish rubbed
so the wood shines and
smells like strange waxy lemons.
Sweeping and vacuuming
deep under furniture,
removing fingerprints from windows,
sweeping the stairs clean.

Kitchen shelves straightened,
each cup and plate set in place,
in the order of who gets up first.
The sink is scoured and gleams,
no traces of dinner or Ajax left.
A new white stove, burners scrubbed,
waits at the ready, no matches needed
to fire up this model, just turn the knobs.
Still, we can't gather to warm feet or heat
bricks for beds by the oven door anymore.

The future will come,
tear out the pantry,
put in a half-bath,
replace wainscoting with
tile, remove the radio
from on top of the fridge.
There will be formica counters,
cabinets for the mixer and bowl to
blend volumes of bread dough in.
The new refrigerator will be large.
You won't use the cold room
for keeping food anymore.

Canning Jars

I had need of the old jars this morning,
went to the cellar to retrieve them.
The canning jars still held bits
of your faded handwriting.

Twenty-two years ago you wrote
lavender, thyme, anise hyssop
on stickers with neat calligraphy,
a row of garden for the herb shelf.

It was difficult to loosen faded labels,
to fill the jars with something new.
They now sparkle in the dish drainer,
aside from rust on the hinges.

Like what changes the heart
what changes iron to rust
can't be removed easily.

Hye Holiday Gathering

Gram prepared paklava and bourma without
a written recipe. Like a newly hatched bird
I waited for bits of sweetness to fall,
walnuts covered with cinnamon, honey
mixed with lemon. I stood on a stool to watch.
Before me, Hrpesima, Anoush, and Mariam had
rolled it by hand, but when I was six we bought
paper-thin phyllo from Sevan's Market in Watertown.

Gram melted butter in the cast iron skillet.
Don't let the butter sizzle–too hot!
She mixed sugar and cinnamon in a bowl for me to add,
got out the heavy rolling pin, and I crushed
walnuts beneath its weight. Gram said *be sure
the nuts are ground fine! Grind them again—
No, still too big.* I pushed the rolling pin hard against
walnuts, and we mixed in sugar and cinnamon.

We took one layer of phyllo at a time,
brushed with melted butter, sprinkled in nuts,
then rolled as quickly as we could.
Finally, using the sharpest blade,
we sliced the fragile rolls and
placed them on the baking sheet.
Hers were straight and long,
mine crinkled, like thin fabric.

I have the recipe still, yellowed with age,
thin and tattered, like phyllo dough,
filled with handed-down memories from those
who sat at this table before me —Shushan, Bedros,
Kevont, Katchador, Sitanoush, all cooking and eating
to honor Harput, our homeland no longer on the map.
I'm the old one now. When I cook,
grandmother's voice follows me, step by step.

Nesselrode Pudding

My dad tasted Nesselrode Pudding
on their New York honeymoon
back in the 40s at the Taft Hotel.
Delicious, light as air, he said.

Cooking for others can be
a lot like prayer, the settling
in to a quiet mind, eliminating
distractions, imagining contentment
arriving on a plate through alchemy
of mixing, heating, spices and love.

When I was twelve I found
recipes for the pudding
and cooked them one by one,
offered them up at supper time.
I remember egg whites

that rose like clouds, whipped yolks
and sugar transformed to golden foam.
I worked for a smile to reach his eyes.
But what does a 12 year-old know
of honeymoons and hope?

June Morning

The first warm June morning
I gather rhubarb and wild
strawberries that perfume the air.
Sweeter than any garden berry,
four would fill a thimble.

Back at the kitchen counter
I slice pale rhubarb stalks,
eight cups worth, into the pot,
add sugar, cardamon, and vanilla.

Some things are constant in our lives,
like stirring at a stove on a spring morning.
Crisp stalks of burgundy transform to silk.
Grandmother, mother, and now me,
we've all stirred at the stove for love.

Refugees from Endearments

For David, who asked if I could translate his grandfather's words.

He always wondered
what endearments Grandfather
had uttered in the language
he didn't understand.

His grandfather commanded attention
with blue eyes that noticed everything.
Torn from Hye mountains near Harput,
he settled in the foothills near Albany.

Grandfather planted string beans
and cabbages each spring,
cherished the grape leaves rather
than the purple globed fruits.

Cleaned up and on best behavior,
his family drove up to visit.
Dressed in church clothes, they'd
changed into play clothes later.

When Grandfather stepped on the porch
to proclaim dinner, he'd appraise them
when they tumbled up the porch steps
to wash hands at the kitchen sink.

He'd watch with piercing eyes
and pronounced *tutum golukh,*
as they scrambled into the kitchen
tucking in their shirttails.

This endearment still stayed
with him forty years later.
It didn't matter what the words meant,
just that they were endearments.

These Armenian words traveled
to New England with refugees
that settled here, endearments that
had grown rusty from disuse.

Now he was settled with family
of his own, and found another child
of survivors from that distant village
who knew the dialect and translated.

Ah yes.   *I know that phrase well.*
My grandmother often said that to me.
Tutum golukh—pumpkin head,
foolish   empty   like a gourd.

Remember, in our culture, you don't want
to draw too much attention to what is precious.

October

A maple by the porch turns
yellow, orange, and red
before leaves
tumble
        and
                dry.

Weeds fade to

        pale yellow

                burgundy

                      lavender.

The last apples hang ripe, softening.
Intoxicated honeybees
devour them.

October plays

        with dark and light

                shadow and color.

Wind tosses falling leaves, the butterflies of autumn.

Chipmunks and bluejays
rob the compost heap.
When I put the garden to bed
the last crickets sing.

What She Saved

after Heritage, by Joelle Taylor
For my mother, Anna

It is said when they opened her
first they found a snowstorm
from December 14, 1946,
when she married John in the Sacred
Heart Church. There was the feather
from her hat, a high-heeled pump,
an old corsage and menu
from their honeymoon in New York.

Further down there were bits of flannel,
lace, a small sewing machine that
whirred, making new clothes
from someone's bigger ones,
stitching nightgowns cut from worn
sheets, tiny shirts from bigger ones.

There were walking shoes,
a baby carriage that held
two of us when the walk was too long.
Tucked away were squares of fudge that sold
for two cents at the Jewish bakery we passed,
tattered recipes, oatmeal, walnuts,
fresh squeezed oranges, a sack of flour set
on a kitchen table, and our old stove heating up.
There was a radio on, maybe Count Basie playing,
or Tony Bennett crooning from the top of the refrigerator.

Last, there were purple lilacs that grew at the front door,
and roses from the front garden that John grew for her.

An Early Snow

An early boon from winter

this hushed morning

no crows

    no squirrels

        no owls hunting

heavy snows are coming

  will weigh down branches

  block roads   break electric lines

we fill pitchers with water

bring in firewood   gather kindling

put shovel and sled at the doorway.

now we wait

    watch from the window

        for the first snowflakes to fall

Traveling through Marseille 1915

It began with conflict, hunger,
and fathers dragged from homes.
It continued with worry and waiting,
mothers sewing coins into clothes
for when they left home.

Finally Uncle arrived with passports.
Children would leave first.
The key to survival, arranged marriages
that allowed entrance into the US, finally
in place. But it had taken too long.

The village was attacked a day
before their leaving. Men and boys
dragged to the church, locked in
and set aflame. Women and babies
bled into the soil that afternoon.
Survivors were marched
from Harput to Aleppo
until they were too tired
and hungry to go on.

A ship from Marseille gave passage
to arranged marriages that unlocked
America's door. Family survives
in stories, and in each day of living,
of not being hungry anymore.

Thanksgiving Choreg

Sleep and stillness cling to my eyes.
Morning light trickles through pine branches
into the kitchen where yeast-raised
soft pillows of dough rise overnight.
I slide the fragrance of warm yeast
into the waiting oven.

I kept the wood stove on last night
to coddle the dough,
to be kind to myself.
Now I sit at the window as fog lifts
in soft wisps and sip tea.

The world here is quiet, aside
from a faucet dripping and the ping
of the oven as it heats.
Strong tea mingles with the aroma
of rising dough.
Do we not all rise with some redemption,
new each morning?

In other homes people move
toward family gatherings
or wake in a jumble of legs and arms
in unfamiliar beds,
while I sit with my ancestors
baking this bread.

I receive the old ones
and the fragrance and the taste.
I listen to the small kitchen sounds
against the quiet outside—
the complete stillness of each branch and leaf,
the warm cup in my hand.

Midnight Hunger

Baby owls screech
demanding to be fed.
They remind me of my own
colicky infant who needed
to be held during
the darkest night hours,
whose cries pierced my heart
with midnight hunger.

I'm drawn from bed to the window
by howls and listen as owlets
pierce my heart again.

When grey light leaks
into day a mother owl
captures a squirrel so heavy
she can't fly back to the nest.
She flutters in short hops before
vanishing into the pines.
Later, I find her wing imprints
where she brushed against snow.

Quince Preserves

We were surprised to find this Armenian
treasure on our first visit to my Irish
godfather's new home in Woburn,
a world away from our East Cambridge street.

Beyond the tumbled stone wall we passed
into an orchard, and entered Eden. It wasn't
only the children that gaped with wonder.
The grownups fell silent, too.

How quickly the old country can resurrect
in our hearts. For Dad and Jimmy Sullivan,
the Irish countryside rose like a captured
bird who discovers an open window.

Gram's home in 1912 Harput rose like
an apparition. Her childhood farm
lay before her for a moment out of time,
and fragrance of quince filled her.

Gram picked three quince from Jimmy Sullivan's tree.
He gave her more. Jimmy's own kids were running around
like banshees. We hadn't ever had that much space to run
together—and we didn't know what do to with it.

The next morning Gram prepared quince. She washed
the fruits, scraped away the furry coating, sliced
through hardness, working alone, except for me,
watching. She inhaled fragrance as she stirred.

White quince softened into gold. Jars of fruit
were suspended in light, preserved.

Late August

I sit on porch steps,
watch the sun burn
off the late August dew.
Fog fronds curl away
from Brown-Eyed Susans
and squash flowers.

I sip tea and watch bumblebees
already working. They hover and dip
into each separate chive blossom,
feet first, bury their heads
deep in its glory. Orange pollen sacs
fill on their back legs, travelers
with tiny brocade carpet bags.

I move close, follow their progress
as they make morning music, moving
to purple thyme and oregano. Buzzing,
clicks when grasshoppers jump,
wings spread wide,
and cricket song,
all before the sun heats the day.

Keep In Mind
> *For Reverend Nshan Khevont Kilarjian, always in my heart.*

Keep in mind, I'm not a historian.

Nshan was born in Parchanj when walled vineyards were ripe
with red Yenour grapes. Soon he learned to climb the mulberry tree,
shake ripe fruit for his sisters to gather to sweetness for winter.

When he turned ten Nshan was sent to school
ten miles from home. He was there when his village was massacred.
French monks hid him, kept him as their own.

> That is to say, most of his family was killed. Girl cousins survived
> a death march from their mountain, across deserts. Three made
> their way to Marseilles, Boston, and Fresno. A toddler was hidden
> by Turkish neighbors who disguised her as their own young boy.

Nshan, now a child of monks, grew up in monasteries.
After the Armistice he traveled to Venice where he studied
another seven years. He was ordained a doctor, a Vartabed,
and moved to Crete, worked as a traveling missionary
and teacher, partnered with a donkey in the dry hills.

> When he was young Nshan picked apricots with his mother,
> put them in baskets to dry for winter. He loved the kitchen
> spices and smells, the warmth, how his family gathered
> to hear stories, how good being in the lap of love felt.

I am not a historian, but I know how he loved.
I know he returned to the monastery in Venice,
helped others find their way. From leading a donkey
over mountains he became an aide to Pope Pius XII.

> Nshan lived at the Vatican, but always searched
> for family that may have survived. Nshan found us
> when I was five. When the doorbell rang and
> Gram opened the door, tears fell with their embrace.
> I knew this was what a grandfather would be like,
> just like him, when he hugged me and held me close.

Elaine is a writer, herbalist, and artist. She's worked as an environmental educator, early childhood educator, and an English as a Second Language teacher as well. Her first chapbook, *The Heart is a Nursery For Hope*, won first honors from Flutter Press in 2016, and her second chapbook, *Look Behind You*, was published in late 2019 by Flutter Press. Most recently Elaine's work was published in *The Common, Pensive Journal, Culinary Origami*, and similar journals. These poems are written from her Armenian family stories. They echo stories of many refugees and immigrants from many lands who have survived hardship and continued on. *http://elainereardon.wordpress.com.*

Milton Keynes UK
Ingram Content Group UK Ltd.
UKHW040745261024
450281UK00006B/58